T R U
L I V E

Captain
James Cook

OXFORD

UNIVERSITY PRESS

Great Clarendon Street, Oxford OX2 6DP

Oxford University Press is a department of the University of Oxford.
It furthers the University's objective of excellence in research, scholarship,
and education by publishing worldwide in

Oxford   New York
Auckland   Cape Town   Dar es Salaam   Hong Kong   Karachi
Kuala Lumpur   Madrid   Melbourne   Mexico City   Nairobi
New Delhi   Shanghai   Taipei   Toronto

With offices in
Argentina   Austria   Brazil   Chile   Czech Republic   France   Greece
Guatemala   Hungary   Italy   Japan   Poland   Portugal   Singapore
South Korea   Switzerland   Thailand   Turkey   Ukraine   Vietnam

Oxford is a registered trade mark of Oxford University Press
in the UK and certain other countries

Text © Haydn Middleton 1997
Illustrations © Oxford University Press 1997

First published 1997
This edition published 2009

A CIP catalogue record for this book is available from the British Library

ISBN: 978-0-19-911960-8

1 3 5 7 9 10 8 6 4 2

Paper used in the production of this book is a natural,
recyclable product made from wood grown in sustainable forests.
The manufacturing process conforms to the environmental
regulations of the country of origin.

Printed in China

TRUE LIVES

Captain James Cook

Illustrated by Alan Marks

Haydn Middleton

OXFORD

James Cook was born in 1728, in the village of Marton in the north of England. His family did farm work, and they lived in a small cottage with earth walls on the edge of the Yorkshire moors.

As James grew up, he helped on the farm. But he also learned to read and write, and became very good at arithmetic. When he had any free time, he went down to the coast to watch the ships passing by. They were carrying coal down to London, where King George II had his court.

James loved to gaze out to sea. His secret dream was to be a sailor. He longed to visit London, and cities in foreign countries as well. Perhaps he might even travel on a ship to lands that nobody yet knew about.

At the age of seventeen, James went out to work. He became a shop-assistant in the nearby village of Staithes, selling groceries and "haberdashery", or sewing materials.

This was a good job for a farm boy, and James worked hard. He did not say much, so people never really knew what he was thinking. He seemed happy enough in the shop, but in his heart he still wanted to go to sea.

James read every book he could
find about the world's great oceans.
European seamen had been making
maps of the Atlantic Ocean for centuries.
But to James's surprise, the huge Pacific
Ocean was still a mystery. Some geographers
believed that a continent full of people existed
down there. They thought that it "balanced out" all
the land at the top of the world.

When James was eighteen, he decided to follow his dream. He gave up his job at the shop and became an apprentice to John Walker, a coal-ship owner at the local port of Whitby. At last he was going to sea – as a Ship's Boy.

James was big and strong for his age. He also had to be brave, because life on the coal ships could be tough and dangerous. But James loved every minute of it, and between voyages he read book after book about "navigation", the science of keeping ships on course.

John Walker was pleased with James – he was always so calm and reliable. In 1755 he asked James to take command of a coal ship. But James had other plans. Britain was about to fight a war against France. James joined the Navy, and three years later he was crossing the Atlantic Ocean to Canada as Ship's Master, in charge of navigation on *HMS Pembroke*.

Britain and France were countries in Europe. But they also ruled over empires made up of lands in other continents. They were fighting now about who should rule Canada.

One dark night in 1759, James had a vital job to do. Ships carrying British soldiers were sailing up Canada's St Lawrence River. They planned to make a surprise attack on the great French fortress of Quebec. James, the expert navigator, had to map out a safe path for the warships to follow.

This was not easy. The river was wide, fast-flowing and full of rocks. But James calmly guided all the soldiers as far as Quebec. There they rushed ashore, captured the fortress, then went on to seize the whole of Canada. James's map of the St Lawrence River was so good, people were still using it a hundred years later.

After the war James returned to London. He was now 34 years old. Most men of that age were already married. James had been so busy since joining the Navy, there had been no time to find a wife.

In 1762 James married a woman called Elizabeth Batts, the daughter of a shopkeeper. They set up home together and soon started a family. But James was hardly ever at home. He spent the next five summers far across the Atlantic Ocean, making detailed maps of Canada's coastlines for the Navy.

Then in 1768 James was finally given command of his own vessel – *HMS Endeavour*. It had once been a coal ship, so James knew exactly how to sail it. His masters in the Navy had decided that he was ready for a very special mission. They were sending him into the vast, little-known Pacific Ocean.

The *Endeavour* set sail from Plymouth on 26 August 1768. The ship was only 32 metres long, but it had to carry ninety-four men. Some of them were famous scientists. They hoped to sail to the Pacific island of Tahiti. There they would watch the "Transit of Venus" – the movement of the planet Venus across the Sun. That was the official purpose of the expedition.

But James also had some secret orders. He was to search for the Great Southern Continent, which no European had ever found.

It was a difficult voyage for everyone on board. But at last on 13 April 1769 James guided the ship safely into Matavai Bay, Tahiti, in good time for the scientists to see the Transit. Luckily, the native people of Tahiti were very friendly. James enjoyed getting to know their customs. But on 13 July 1769 it was time to move on – into the unknown.

The *Endeavour* sailed west then south. After three months, a large mass of land loomed ahead. It was New Zealand, which had first been seen by Dutch sailors in 1642. Was this a part of a Great Southern Continent? Before James could find out, the local people – the Maoris – made a fierce attack on the *Endeavour*.

Endeavour's crew managed to beat off the Maori war canoes, but they had to stay on constant alert for more attacks. James was unafraid. He took the ship carefully along the coasts, making a map as he went. New Zealand turned out to be made up of two islands.

Heading west again, James found another shore and began to map it. One place was so full of new plants he called it Botany Bay (botany is the study of plants). His men also spotted some strange hopping animals – kangaroos. James called this wonderful land New South Wales, because it reminded him of Wales in Britain. Later, it would be known as Australia.

It was not easy to sail along Australia's eastern coast. One night, the ship came to a juddering halt. Terrible cracking noises filled the air. The *Endeavour* had run into a reef: a great ridge of coral just under the water.

Panic broke out as the ship started to sink. But James kept his nerve. Calmly he told his men how to shift the ship off the reef. Then they stretched a sail over the hole that was letting in water, and sailed to a safe beach to repair it.

When the hole was mended, the *Endeavour* sailed back home to England. The expedition had lasted for three years. Usually on long voyages, many men died of a disease called scurvy, caused by their poor diet. But James had provided healthy food, so his crew was not badly affected.

The voyage had been a huge success. James's report of it made him very famous. Soon New Zealand and Australia were added to the British Empire. But still no one knew for sure if a Great Southern Continent existed.

AUSTRALIA

'Endeavour' ran aground here

NEW ZEALAND

J ames spent only a year at home with his family. He was promoted again, to Commander, and in July 1772 he set out on a second voyage. Again his mission was to find out if there really was a Great Southern Continent. This time there were two ships. James commanded the *Resolution*. Tobias Furneaux was in charge of the *Adventure*.

The two ships called at Cape Town in southern Africa, then headed off in search of the southern continent. But the further south they sailed, the worse the weather became. The crews had never known such cold – even the special warm clothing that James had brought for them did not keep out the chill.

The ships zigzagged past huge icebergs until at last a great sea of ice blocked their path. James now knew the truth. If a southern continent existed, it could only be in these frozen wastes known as the "Antarctic" – and no people could possibly live there.

The *Resolution* and the *Adventure* went on to map over thirty new islands in the South Pacific. As they did so, they lost contact with each other.

James and his crew were glad to be back in the warm ocean after almost freezing in their search for the southern continent. One of the most mysterious places they visited was Easter Island. On the grassy slopes of this lonely island, massive stone heads had been carved. Some of them were over nine metres tall. Nobody knew what they were for.

When the *Resolution* reached Tahiti, the island's big war fleet put on a show. The Tahitians, like most of the islanders in the Pacific, were friendly to the British sailors. But the Melanesians at Erromanga threw stones and fired arrows. And in New Zealand, James found that something much worse had happened to some of the *Adventure*'s crew.

The *Resolution* called in at New Zealand on its way home. There James was horrified to learn that ten crewmen from the *Adventure* had been killed in a fight with the Maoris. The *Adventure* had then returned to England, becoming the first ship ever to sail around the world from west to east.

James and his men followed in the *Resolution*. Throughout this voyage they were able to stay on course more accurately than ever before, because James had brought along a brand new piece of equipment to help him navigate.

This was a "chronometer", a sea clock invented by John Harrison. The Navy had asked James to test it, and he found that it was very accurate. He called it his "Watch Machine, our never failing guide". It guided James and the *Resolution* back to England in July 1775. There he was met with a hero's welcome.

Route of Cook's second voyage

James had been ill for a while on the second voyage. He was now 46, which was quite old in those days. And he had spent seven of the last eight years at sea. He believed that his days of adventure were over, and planned to spend the rest of his life quietly with his wife and three children.

He was well rewarded for his explorations. He was promoted to "Captain" Cook. The Royal Society – an important club for scientists – made him a member. He was even invited to court, where he was presented to King George III.

Then in 1776, the Navy organized a new expedition. Its aim was to see if there was a "North-West Passage", or route from the Pacific to the Atlantic across the top of America. The Earl of Sandwich asked James who he thought should be put in command. James smiled and said he would do the job himself.

In July 1776, the *Resolution* set sail from Plymouth. James called his ship "A Noah's Ark". On board were all sorts of farm animals, to be used for breeding in faraway lands. A second ship, the *Discovery*, was commanded by Charles Clerke.

They went first to New Zealand. James left some rabbits and goats with the Maoris. Then he moved on to Tahiti, and afterwards the Hawaiian Islands, which he had not visited before. The people there greeted him warmly.

In March 1778 James and his crews reached North America's Pacific coast. They followed it northwards, making maps as they went, and meeting with many different tribes of Native American people. But finally thick ice barred their way. James had to admit it: there was no North-West Passage, just as there had been no Great Southern Continent.

The *Resolution* and *Discovery* now had to turn and head back south. James remembered how friendly the people of Hawaii had been. He decided to call there again. The two ships arrived in January 1779.

But this time the Hawaiians were in a different mood. They kept picking quarrels with the crews and stealing their belongings. James was furious. On 14 February he tried to sort out the trouble on his own, at Kealakekua Bay. The Hawaiians were confused. They panicked, surrounded James, then attacked him. When they stepped away, Captain Cook was dead.

James once wrote that he wanted "to go as far as it is possible for man to go". On his three great voyages of exploration, he went further than any other man of his time. He helped to complete the map of the world.

Today there are still places named after him in Alaska, Australia, New Zealand and Polynesia.

Cook Inlet

PACIFIC OCEAN

Cook Islands

Mount Cook

Cook Strait

Important dates in Captain Cook's life

1728 James Cook born in Marton, England.

1746 James becomes a ship's boy on a coal ship.

1755 James leaves the coal ships to join the Royal Navy.

1759 James's charts of the St Lawrence River help win the battle for Quebec.

1762 James marries Elizabeth Batts.

1768–70 On his first major voyage, James visits Tahiti and charts coasts of New Zealand and Australia.

1772–75 On his second voyage, James sights Antarctica and tests the chronometer.

1776–79 James's final voyage, to look for a north-west passage around America.

1779 James killed by angry Hawaiians in Kealakekua Bay.

Index